All in the Mind

Books are to be returned on or before
the last date below.

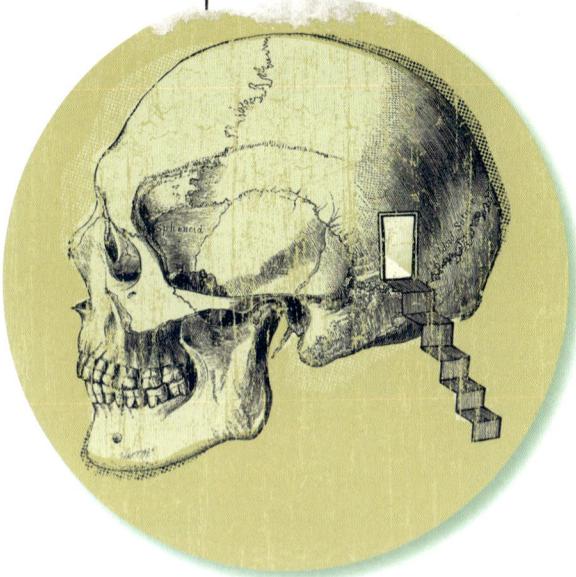

Badger Publishing Limited
Oldmedow Road,
Hardwick Industrial Estate,
King's Lynn PE30 4JJ
Telephone: 01438 791037

www.badgerlearning.co.uk

4 6 8 10 9 7 5 3

All in the Mind ISBN 978-1-78464-138-2

Publisher: Susan Ross
Senior Editor: Danny Pearson
Publishing Assistant: Claire Morgan
Designer: Cathryn Gilbert
Series Consultant: Dee Reid
Copyeditor: Cheryl Lanyon

Photos: Cover Image: © ImageZoo/Alamy
Page 4: © caia image/Alamy
Page 5: © chatchai surakram/Alamy
Page 9: © PhotoAlto/Alamy
Page 10: Jon Brenneis/Getty Images
Page 11: Sam Peet
Page 13: © Purestock/Alamy
Page 14: © Pictorial Press Ltd/Alamy
Page 20: History of American Psychology/University of Akron/Popular Mechanics
Page 21: © Glasshouse Images/Alamy
Page 23: © SuperStock/Alamy
Page 24: © croftsphoto/Alamy
Page 25: © WENN Ltd/Alamy
Page 26: © powys photo/Alamy
Page 28: RUSSELLTATEdotCOM/Getty Images
Page 29: © Alistair Cotton/Alamy

Attempts to contact all copyright holders have been made.
If any omitted would care to contact Badger Learning, we will be happy to make appropriate arrangements.

All in the Mind

Contents

Badger
L E A R N I N G

Vocabulary

behaviour

Cerebellum

conditioning

coordination

Occipital lobe

Parietal lobe

prejudice

psychology

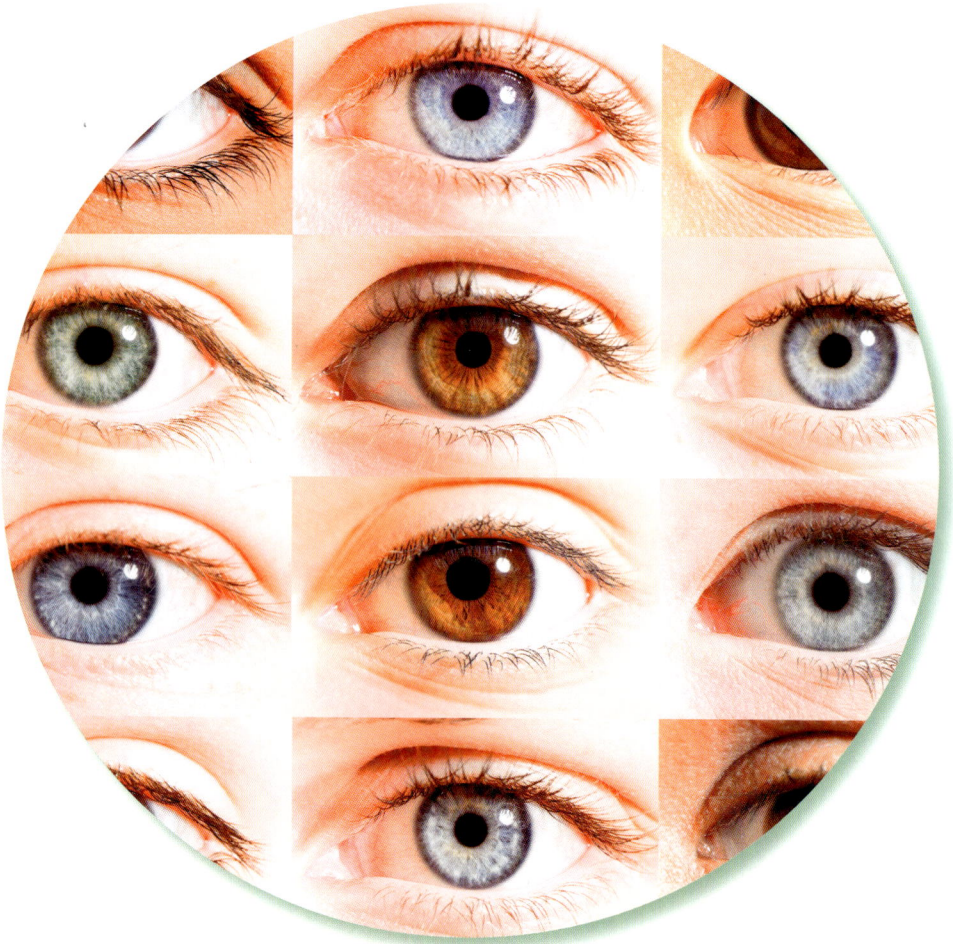

1. The human brain

There are lots of things that we still don't fully understand about the brain, such as:

- What makes us like or dislike things.
- How much of our personality we are born with, and how much of it is shaped by our lives.
- Whether we can trust our memories.
- How we decide the difference between right and wrong.

Our brains control everything we do. Different parts of the brain control different bodily functions.

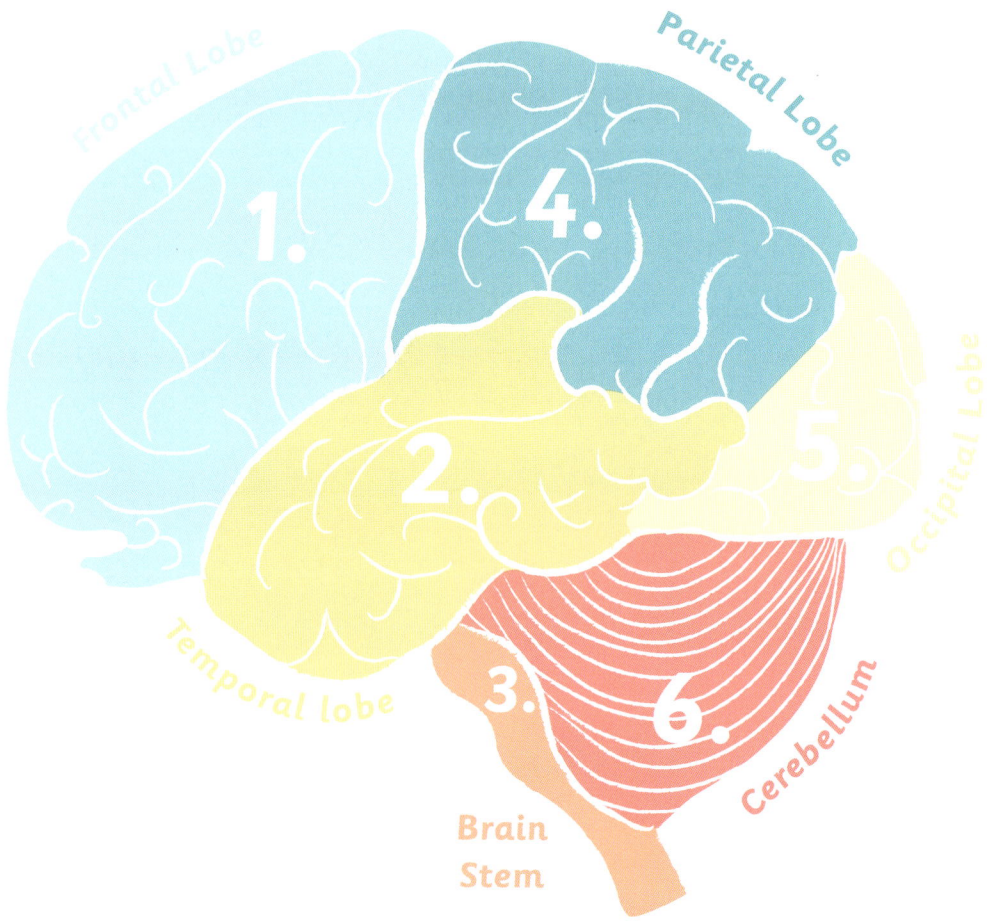

Frontal Lobe

Parietal Lobe

Occcipital Lobe

1.

4.

2.

5.

Temporal lobe

3.

6.

Cerebellum

Brain Stem

1. Frontal lobe – thinking, memory, behaviour and movement.

2. Temporal lobe – hearing, learning and feelings.

3. Brain stem – breathing, heart rate and temperature.

4. Parietal (pa-**rye**-it-ul) lobe – language and touch.

5. Occipital (ox-**sip**-it-ul) lobe – sight.

6. Cerebellum (sarah-**bell**-um) – balance and coordination.

WOW! facts

The human brain contains 400 miles of blood vessels!

Psychology is the study of the human mind and how it behaves in different situations.

Psychologists do experiments to find out more about the human mind. They often go like this:

people are chosen

they are put into two groups

**both groups are asked
to do the same thing**

**the psychologist slightly changes
the conditions of one group – such as
playing music to them**

**the psychologist will try to tell what
difference that small change makes, by
looking at results from both groups**

The group which has no change made is called a control group.

To compare the results of the change, the psychologist needs to make sure there are no other differences between the two groups.

What does the psychologist do to make sure the groups are the same?

- Chooses people of the same age.
- Chooses people with the same background.
- Makes sure the experiments happen in the same place.
- Makes sure the same length of time is spent on both groups.

Experiments done in this way have helped us discover some really interesting things about the human mind.

2. Experiments on children

One type of psychology is called behaviourism. Psychologists who are behaviourists say that all our actions are caused by the experiences we have in our lives.

Some experiments have been done on children to try to show this:

The Bobo doll experiment

Date: 1961

Psychologist: Albert Bandura

Experiment: Do people copy each other or do they behave the way they do because it's who they are?

Number of groups: Three

Group 1: 24 boys and girls aged between three and six were shown an adult being aggressive towards a blow-up doll.

Group 2: 24 boys and girls aged between three and six were shown an adult playing quietly near a blow-up doll.

Group 3: 24 boys and girls aged between three and six were not shown anything at all. This was the control group.

Then the children were let into the room with the doll one at a time and the psychologist watched to see what they would do. What do you think happened?

The group who had seen the adult being aggressive towards the doll were much more likely to also be aggressive towards the doll than the children from both other groups.

These results supported (backed up) Bandura's theory that humans learn behaviour by watching others.

Little Albert

Date: 1920

Psychologist: John Watson

Experiment: Do we link scary and non-scary experiences in our minds, if they happen at the same time?

People in the experiment: One nine-month-old baby called 'Little Albert'.

1. Watson showed Albert a white rat.

2. Albert was allowed to touch the rat. He showed no fear of the rat at all.

3. Later, Watson showed Albert the rat again. But this time Watson made a really loud noise behind Albert's back. Albert began to cry.

4. After a while, when Watson showed Albert the rat, Albert started crying – even if there was no loud noise.

These results supported Watson's theory that we can be taught or 'conditioned' to link things together. Albert linked the rat with the scary loud noise.

WOW! facts

Ivan Pavlov had already done a 'conditioning' experiment like this in 1890. He rang a bell every time he gave his dogs food. Soon the dogs started drooling whenever they heard the bell, even if they couldn't see any food.

The Robber's Cave experiment

Date: 1954

Psychologist: Muzafer Sherif

Experiment: Are people more aggressive when they are in a group competing with another group?

Number of groups: Two

Each group had 11 boys in it. Each group had its own camp and, at first, the groups didn't know about each other.

Then Muzafer made the groups compete with each other at games. The winning group got prizes.
The losing group had to wait longer for their dinner.

Soon there was aggression between the groups.
They called each other names and even stole from each other.

The results of the experiment supported Muzafer's theory that group competition can cause aggression and dislike.

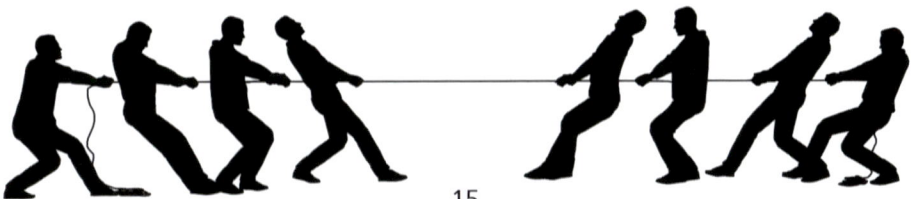

A class divided

Date: 1968

Experimenter: Jane Elliot, a teacher

Experiment: To explain racism.

Number of groups: Two – the blue-eyed children and the brown-eyed children.

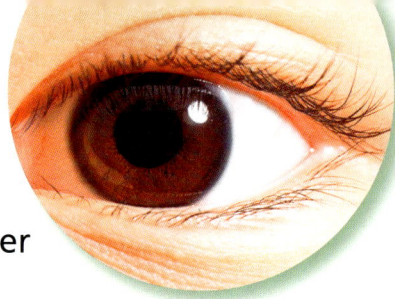

Jane Elliott treated the blue-eyed students much better by giving them rewards and praise. She made the brown-eyed students wear brown collars and sit at the back of the class. They were not even allowed to drink from the same water fountain!

The blue-eyed students started to become bossy and mean towards their classmates – they started to think they were better than them.

The next week Elliot switched the groups around. Then the brown-eyed children started to think they were more important.

This result supported Elliot's theory that group behaviour can create prejudice about differences that do not matter.

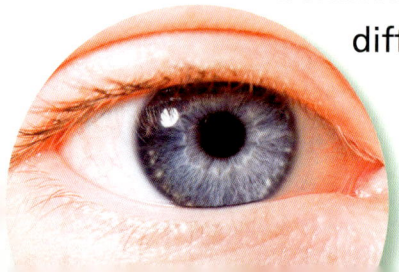

3. Obedience and conformity

Some experiments have been created to show how likely people are to conform (copy or obey others) in certain situations.

The Asch conformity experiment

Date: 1951
Psychologist: Solomon Asch
Experiment: To find out how much a person's opinions can be affected by a group.

One person was put in a room with seven actors. This person did not know what the experiment was for, or that the other people in the room were actors.

A   B   C

The group were then shown three lines and each person in turn had to point out the longest line.

The actors had all been told beforehand to choose one of the shorter lines and say that was the longest.

In the experiment, 75% of the people tested copied the others and chose a line that was obviously not the longest line.

This result supported Asch's theory that people will say something even if they know it is not the truth because they want to fit in with others.

The Milgram experiment

Date: 1963

Psychologist: Stanley Milgram

Experiment: How far will people go to obey an instruction or order?

Number of groups: Two – the teachers and the learners.

People were given roles of 'teacher' and 'learner'. They were put in rooms next to each other. The learner was an actor but the teacher didn't know that. There was also an 'experimenter' dressed in a lab coat who was an actor too.

The teacher had to read out a question. If the learner got it wrong, the teacher had to press a button to give them an electric shock.

The power of the shock had to be greater each time. There were switches marked from 15 volts all the way up to 450 volts (severe shock – danger of death).

The learner was not actually getting an electric shock. But each time the teacher pressed a button, they heard a recording of someone screaming in pain and asking to end the experiment.

If the teacher tried to stop giving shocks the experimenter told them to go on.

Over 50% of the teachers gave electric shocks up to 450 volts, and 100% gave electric shocks up to 300 volts. This result supported Milgram's theory that people will do as they are told even if it means really hurting another person.

WOW! facts

Milgram's results have been used to try to explain the horrific killings by the Nazis in World War Two.

The Stanford Prison experiment

Date: 1971

Psychologist: Philip Zimbardo

Experiment: How does human behaviour change in a prison setting?

Number of groups: Two

Zimbardo set up a mock prison. He got 12 students to pretend to be prisoners and 12 students to pretend be guards for two weeks.

The trouble was, the guards got into their roles a bit too much. They became very aggressive and gave out cruel punishments for not obeying the rules. They often did not let prisoners:

- eat
- wash themselves
- go to the toilet

Many prisoners had breakdowns.

This result supported Zimbardo's theory that different roles and surroundings can change the way we behave.

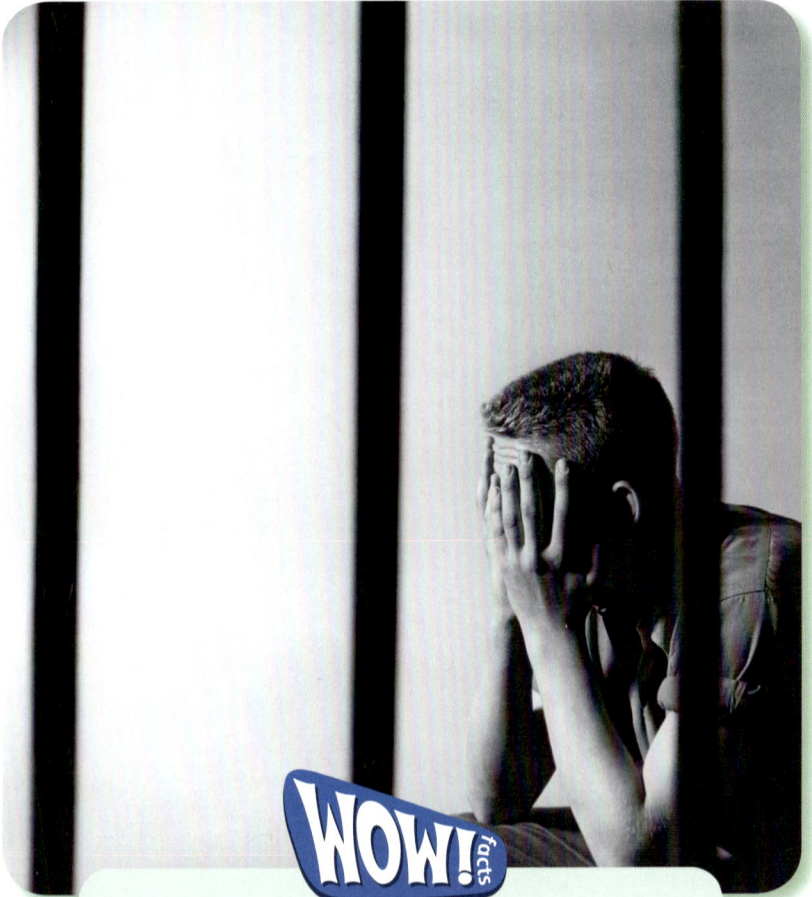

WOW! facts

The students pretending to be prisoners were so upset at how they were treated that Zimbardo had to call off the experiment after only six days.

4. Getting involved

You might think that if you were in any kind of trouble it would be best to be in a crowded place. You'd feel there was more chance of someone coming to help you. But this isn't true.

Psychologists describe something called the bystander effect. This says that someone is more likely to help you if there are fewer people around. But if you are in a crowded place, most people think that someone else will stop and help you, so they carry on.

What's it worth?

People pay hundreds of dollars to hear world-famous violinist Joshua Bell play.

In 2007, he did an experiment to see whether people would pay that much money to hear him play if he was not in a concert hall, but just busking on the street.

Very few people stopped to listen to him play when he was busking and he only made $32 the whole day. This experiment shows how different surroundings affect how we react to the things in front of us.

Missing child

Do you think you are quite good at noticing things?

One clever experiment shows we may not be as good at noticing things as we think we are.

A poster of a missing child was put up in a public place. Lots of people stopped to look at the poster but no one noticed that the child in the picture was standing nearby.

5. Memory

Do you think you have a good memory?

Another clever experiment shows that what we remember may not be what actually happened.

The Loftus and Palmer Experiment

Date: 1974

Psychologists: Elizabeth Loftus and John Palmer

Experiment: Can we trust people's memories?

Groups: Five groups of nine students.

All the groups watched the same film of a car accident. Then they were asked this question:

> **How fast were the cars going when they _____ each other?**

Each group was given a different word to describe the crash:

- contacted
- hit
- bumped
- collided
- smashed

contacted

hit

bumped

collided

smashed

What do you think happened?

The more violent the word was, the higher the guesses were. The group who were given the word 'smashed' to describe the crash guessed that the cars were going much faster than the group who were given the word 'contacted'.

This result supported Loftus's theory that we cannot always trust our memories. They can change after the event has happened and we might not even know it!

6. Is it OK to mess with people's minds?

Some of the older experiments in this book would NOT be allowed today.

Today, there are rules called 'ethics' to protect people who take part in experiments:

The people in the experiment must agree to take part and must be told what the experiment is about.

Nobody can get hurt in an experiment – mentally or physically.

People must be allowed to leave the experiment any time they like.

So, if a psychologist asked you to take part in an experiment, would you say yes?

Questions

Which part of the brain controls memory? (*page 7*)

What is a control group? (*page 8*)

What did Jane Elliot try to teach her students about? (*page 16*)

How long did Zimbardo's prison experiment last for? (*page 23*)

What is the bystander effect? (*page 24*)

What did Joshua Bell find out about his violin playing? (*page 25*)

Index